Messages on the Water

Poems by Merrijane Rice

Acknowledgements for the previous publishing of some of these poems are due to *Chapparral Poetry Forum, Davis County Clipper, Encore, Ensign, Mormon Artist, Panorama, Poet Tree, Segullah, Utah Sings, Utah Voices & Poetry On Canvas*, and *Wildnerness Interface Zone*.

ISBN: 978-1-387-25071-4

Cover illustration: *A Hundred Years Downstream* by Merrijane and Nathan Rice

Interior illustrations: *Paper Boats* by Merrijane and Nathan Rice

Printed by Lulu.com Publishing

For my family

everywhere

Thank You ...

To Jason, Parker, Nathan, Joshua, and Jacob for inspiring me.

To Nathan for helping with the illustrations.

To Kathy Cowley for cheerleading and helping with poem selection, editing, and arrangement.

To the Utah State Poetry Society for providing hundreds of hours of critiquing, education, and support over the years.

Contents

Faith

Gifts

Nature

Family

Faith

From the East

It almost feels like fate,
and yet I know it isn't.
Just a chain of choices
long as life itself—

this I say, this not;
this I do, this not;
this I study, ponder,
believe—

until by twists and turns
I arrive here
to gaze upward at a new light
in heaven's velvet veil,
a tear where God streams through
like lightning from a pinprick
or revelation from a whisper,
calling *follow*.

It's another step
in the long progression,
one more choice:

stay a scholar only,
seeking and sorting ancient tales
in dark-paneled, perfumed rooms,
safely conjuring heaven,
ever learning but never knowing

or gather my gifts quickly,
run toward the heart-thumping
pull of prophecy,
swing from stirrup to saddle
in a smooth leap,
and leave tonight to follow
the Star.

Numberless

… Now, for this cause I know
that man is nothing,
which thing I never had supposed.
> *Moses 1:10*

I am a dust mote in a ribbon of light
for a moment bright like a tiny star
scarcely aware of whose breath
stirred me swirling in this cloud
or set me adrift among billions
sifting to the window sill

but I know something
of reflected glory
of dancing in the sun
of buoyant hope that He
who numbers the sands of the sea
will count me in

The Other Virgin

Yes, there were ten virgins—
five wise with lamps and vessels
full to last till midnight,
and five foolish who slept empty,
resting too soundly,
too comfortably to even
shift positions.

Then there's you,
outside the story.
You pour everything in,
burning as fast as drops fall
so you can stay awake all night
to care for others who always need
more than you have to give.

Come, tuck your arm through mine.
Until the call sounds,
we'll share a single light,
praying that the Bridegroom
who multiplies loaves and fishes
and frees springs in the desert
will never let our cruse of oil fail.

On Trial

My optimism vacillates like tides
progressing bit by bit, then falling back.
Old fear reclaims new faith with each attack
and where hope lived, now hopelessness resides.

Shall I, a troubling widow, endless plead
until the weary Judge inclines his ear,
or fill my mouth with arguments sincere,
well ordered to convince him of my need?

Already I've employed a lawyer's skill
in arguing my all-consuming grief.
God knows my need, yet still withholds relief—
can I then turn his mind or change his will?

I must submit, and so amend my plea:
My Father, help me last—put strength in me.

After Eden

As morning overtakes the edge of night
and softens brittle darkness into day,
we stand together in the newborn light
considering what work lies on our way.

An empty field waits quiet in the dawn,
its fresh-plowed furrows stretching out of view.
The labor of a lifetime calls us on
to plant and nourish life while life is new.

Together, then, let's take this challenge up
and press through miles and years on steady feet.
Let heaven's blessings fill our earthly cup
with promises of harvests, rich and sweet.

Until those future fruits, may God provide
our greatest joy in working side by side.

Eve

Sometimes things shout
so soundlessly,
you must listen—
like when fragrant fruit
ripe with promise
hangs within reach,
woos you in capital letters,
JUST ONE BITE.

Then reason hisses:
Wisdom lies
in the hair breadth between
shalt and shalt not.
You could almost fall
into it.

Only hindsight's naked eye
sees what was at stake,
the seam split wide
between life and death.

You'll want to hide,
to crawl between one beat and the next
of your own thudding heart—
but don't.

Instead,
pare out experience.
Carve this lesson in the prints
of your hands and feet:

Eat first to learn hunger.
Hunger will soon teach you
to yearn for bread.

Act II

Today I read about a man who lost
his faith. At once, that traitor fear surprised
my heart, seized hold, and squeezed. I didn't know
the man, his reputation, relatives,
what roadmaps he had pored on to that point.
I only held a pencil sketch in mind—
a rough-drawn scene of inattentive sheep
beset by wolves—that mothers use to warn
their children: safety lies in guarded folds.

His unbelief did not unsteady me.
No—I no longer terrify myself
with indecision. I have made my choice.
Instead, it's for my children that cold fear
rears up and grips me by the throat, tears out
the measured words of reason I should speak.
I pray they never settle for mere roles
in other mothers' moralistic plays
of tragic heroes fallen through self-will.

So, after all, I do know more than just
"A man has lost his faith." I understand
his mother's heart, her disappointed hopes.
I owe her this—to not demean her son
for mine as one more cautionary tale,
but comfort her with this: the play proceeds.
Great falls foreshadow great redemptive deeds.
He may yet recollect, retrace his steps
to find his faith still beating in its place.

Grudge

Like a dragon,
I brood over my false hoard—
sharp, glittering chips
reflect my burning.

Though plated scales armor me,
shattered glass grinds
long, raw gashes
in my soft underbelly.

Guarded and guarding,
I crouch turned in on myself,
chew open old wounds
that should have healed by now.

When will I sweep my tail,
empty this cavern,
and rest on a bare floor
of fresh, clean peace?

In Remembrance

Pain is universal,
pedestrian even.

You walk a strait path,
grasp the iron rod,
skirt precipice edges,

then loss sneaks up,
bayonets from behind,
and saunters off wiping the blade.

In the aftermath,
helpful folks salve your wounds with,
  This happens to everyone.

So you stitch it up clean and tight,
and wait for tides of ache to subside.

But years later,
you sometimes neglect to be careful.
You stretch till the scar
pulls,   *here's where I tore*
twinges, *I wish I'd never*
burns,   *why do I still*

and you wonder,
not if God loves you,
but

if He hung from the cross,
scraping breath after breath,
willing heartbeats just long enough
to heal every unearned sorrow
along with all the world's sins—

if He promised to remember them no more—

  Why can't I forget?

Sleepless Night

I lie awake; my heart is full of pain
that even healing sleep cannot erase.
My knotted thoughts all jostle for a place
within the crowded corners of my brain.

Where lies escape? Will anybody tell
me how to fight this battle to its end?
Will old acquaintances still call me friend
when I have nothing left to give or sell?

Will any brother clear my clouded sight
or any sister smooth my worried brow?
Does anybody care about me now
or wonder if I struggle in the night?

Ten thousand questions trouble me, until
the dawn—then comes the answer: *Peace, be still.*

Hope

It's raining, but the sun is shining through
the clouds and catching prisms from on high.
A stained-glass rainbow stretches 'cross the blue
and gray-domed tabernacle of the sky.

It seems a paradox that rain and sun
should ever meet and mingle in the air
or, stranger, find bright colors in the dun
of dusk to decorate a rainbow there—

for earth-bound lyricists have long rehearsed
how sadness only comes when heaven pours
while sun relieves all cursing from the cursed,
but God evolves our human metaphors.

He makes his own divine analogy
that we with cloudy eyes must learn to see.

Ask, Seek, Knock

A sea of questions fills my mind.
Confusion casts me to and fro.
I pray to leave the storms behind.
Oh Lord, I ask; please help me know.

I stumble through a world of doubt.
Cold mists of darkness keep me blind.
I read to search the answers out.
Oh Lord, I seek; please help me find.

I wander homeless, lonely, poor
throughout a wilderness of sin.
I stand outside thy holy door.
Oh Lord, I knock; please let me in.

Although I struggle in distress,
I know if I will turn to thee,
thy hands await to freely bless.
Oh Lord, I come; draw near to me.

My Father, I Will Cry to Thee

When I go out into the world
to work among my flocks and fields,
for increase and a fruitful yield,
my Father, I will cry to thee.

When I return at each day's end
to rest with family and friends,
my head I'll bow, my knees I'll bend—
my Father, I will cry to thee.

When adversaries stand and fight
to sever me from thy true light,
though battles rage throughout the night,
my Father, I will cry to thee.

My whole life long, my soul I'll bare
with heart drawn out in humble prayer
to ask thee for thy loving care:
My Father, I will cry to thee.

Christmas In Zarahemla

In Zarahemla, all is still
and silent at the setting sun.
The pure in heart are praying for
the sign that Samuel said would come
to Zarahemla on the night that Jesus Christ is born.

In Zarahemla, Nephi bows,
pours out his heart in prayers and tears.
The Lord in mercy reassures:
Lift up your head, be of good cheer,
for Zarahemla, on this night I, Jesus Christ, am born.

In Zarahemla, awe descends
as day continues on through night.
All fall to earth because they know
at last has come the One, True Light.
The Zarahemla sky is bright, for Jesus Christ is born.

In Zarahemla, all is still
and silent at the rising sun.
The pure in heart are full of thanks
and joy because the Savior's come.
Oh Zarahemla, bless this night that Jesus Christ is born!

Three Prayers

Help thou my unbelief; I stand alone
beneath a load of sin and doubt. I grieve,
unsure of how to find my way back home.
But, Lord, my whole soul hungers to believe.

Help thou my growing faith; I follow thee
with hope that every precept, every line
of truth and righteousness will strengthen me
and bring my will in harmony with thine.

Help thou my life-long journey; walk with me.
Thou art my best support, my truest friend.
I strive to mirror thy humility
and walk thy path, enduring to the end.

Old Man

I am the last leaf on the tree, and the wind is blowing.
        Gordon B. Hinckley

Youth is hidden in your skin,
gangly strength in your bones.
Age hangs from you
like a too-large sweater
swaying open as you walk,
showing quicker steps
under the shuffles.
Your eyes glow with quiet fire,
still-burning coals muffled in ash.

One day,
you'll shrug off senescence
like a winter coat,
step out of heavy boot feet,
spring to the flame that lit you,

and I will recognize you
by pictures I glimpsed
around your edges.

Terminal

she wants to die in her sleep

not of starvation—
days to wring out life in bitter trickles
endless knot-fisted hours of regretting
that she didn't say yes
more often

not in a plane crash—
fifteen hovering minutes
to reconsider the road more traveled
before smacking the ocean's face
goodbye

not even by tripping
into an open elevator shaft—
mere seconds to reflect
on graceful free-fall flight
through darkness

she wants to doze in and out
play peek-a-boo with eternity
until she wakes and stretches
wide-eyed behind the curtain

On the Death of a Child

Being a mother also,
I know I can't uproot
the pain planted in your chest
or untangle your frayed thoughts.
I can't sweep the darkness
from under your sheltered edges
or smooth peace over you
like a clean sheet.

But I'll try anyway—
weep with you and mourn awhile,
caress calm into your spent heart,

and remember with you
how David howled for Absalom
and how when the Lord wept
all eternity shook.

Crossing the Waters

In me,
you see a wall—
a basalt cliff unscathed
by churning surf that tosses,
hurls you toward hull breach
against unyielding stone.

But you and I
are one vessel sealed tight,
driven by God's furious wind—

When mountain waves roll you,
I plunge.
When currents wrench your heart,
my timbers groan.
I shudder at each tearing swell
because I know your splintering
sinks us both.

Please,
keep close
through these dark waters.
Believe with me
in a Lord who listens,
who reaches forth to touch
what we hold deep inside
to make it shine.

Refuge

There's a woman across the sea
I've never met—
not in this life.

I imagine she's an early riser,
grateful for pale dawns
flush with peace.
She'd *tsk* my late hibernation,
laughing, *Awake!*
Arise from the dust!

Maybe she has children.
She'd nod and smile when I say
they flood home like a river,
dropping silt past the front door,
spilling downstairs.
She'd lean in close
as we compare hollows carved
by little ones grown
and gone away.

Like me,
she knows the art of waiting
till new faces reveal themselves
as desert or oasis,
wildfire or cool water.

We both wrestle,
wrap ourselves in hope,
cling to deep doctrine
against those who threaten
to rip out root and branch.

But sometimes the Spirit moves us
to faraway places
where promised safety lies
in strange lands.

So when my sister comes
from across the sea,
I will meet her searching—

cushion feet with tender grass,
cover head with untroubled shade,
ease thirst with wellsprings
overflowing.

Christmas Duet

This evening,
Silent Night flows over us.
Your voice scrambles for the tune,
swings wide around the turns
of every verse.
I sing in your ear,
coaxing your notes
into line with mine—

just like before
when we were anonymous angels
jostled by the congregation
in an ocean of murmuring light.
Your hallelujahs broke free,
untethered from a voice
too full to hold the joy.
I drew your tones close to my own,
calmed you with a lullaby.

This evening,
Joy to the World resounds around us.
Hold tight and I will guide again
as we sing what can't be said,
leaving words behind.

Unconditional

I glory in plain-speaking, the austere
and careful art of being understood
and showing through one's words and works the clear
delineation of what's bad and good.

I grasp the opposition in all things,
the need to study out and set apart.
Joy cannot be without matched suffering—
and yet, disquiet murmurs in my heart.

Adept at separation, I lack skill
in making peace with foes, in being one.
Peculiar as I am, I seek God's will,
but can't half emulate the paragon

of One who loves to infinite degree,
who pleads for both my enemy and me.

Volumes

We are brothers and sisters,
I'm told.
And believing,
I've tried to peruse you
like books on a shelf,
to read you through.

But your plots evolve,
shift just beyond
peripheral vision.
I snatch familiar phrases
that seem to mean
different things to you
than to me.

I long for interpreters,
seer stones to focus
ebb and flow of story,
to teach me your arc
and what hopes draw you
toward denouement—
motivations you both hide
and foreshadow.

Yet you escape me.
I sit pondering
your faded illustrations,
searching for family resemblance.

Feast

This apple, wrapped in skin like yellow silk
that brightly shines when rubbed against my sleeve,
has flesh as crisp as linen, fresh as milk,
and sweet to me as sun to greening leaves.

With each refreshing, snapping, dripping bite,
I feel my bleak depression slip away.
My groaning void is filled with summer light
and strength to last another winter day.

The tree that bore this fruit was planted deep
by unknown hands that labored long ago.
My benefactor didn't stay to reap
the harvest, but he taught it how to grow.

Salvation was prepared before my need
because a sower stooped to plant a seed.

Windows of Heaven

When the sky was blue,
my heart was brittle,
dry to blistered souls
seeking drink.

So God hung black clouds low,
let loose His floods,
and poured forth more
than I could hold.

I sputtered and choked—
He wrapped a hand around my heart
and wrung out sustenance
for others.

The sky is gray,
but my heart is soft.
In drier days,
it would have
crumbled.

Gifts

Legacy

Eventually,
everyone is forgotten.

History quickly whittles
Sequoia names
into toothpick clichés:

John Hancock,
Jezebel,
Geronimo.

Heroes and heretics
become trees we can't see
for the forest.

I, too, am a few anecdotes
from annihilation.
Time will wipe me from the slate—

but I carve my petroglyphs and hope
someday you will walk this valley,
read these brittle stick figures,
and clothe their bones in resurrected flesh.

Investing

I gather gold
from groves of autumn aspen,
yellow coins that spin and glint
in quickening wind.

I mine diamonds
from frost-rimed grass,
gray-green blades that shimmer
in sympathy with moon.

I sift through sun-warmed sand
for mother of pearl,
iridescence tucked in mollusk shells
or swirling on surf-churned bubbles.

I tally wealth on paper,
jot measured lines in columns,
sum up treasures of memory
in rows of scanned feet.

When accounting is done,
I give all away,
await the returns.

In the Details

Why do I whittle,
chip old growth from my core,
couple different bits
where wood grains flow
in preordained patterns—

polish glow deep
into knots and grooves
where no probing eye will appraise—

craft precision in knickknacks
that won't be sat on,
eaten from,
or sheltered under?

Because I know Him
who cared to glaze rainbows
on the fractured wings
of a housefly.

Superstitious

When I was small enough
to ride sofa arms like ponies,
chase spring-blown cottonwood fluff,
puzzle over hieroglyphs in the Sunday funnies—

I lived by superstition:
avoided sidewalk cracks like worms after rain,
jinxed my sister when we spoke in unison,
crossed my heart for truth,
crossed fingers for a lie.
Fairies played cricket fiddles
beneath my window,
and leprechauns farmed
four-leaf clovers on the front lawn.

Time's long gone since I sipped tea
from yellow daffodil bowls
or yelled *hello* to my echoes.
The click-clacking engine of adulthood
lured me away, lulled me,
pulled me inch by inch past the point
of warding off the evil eye—

so far that even a world of ogres
can't restore virtue to old talismans.

But Sundays I still wrap myself
in a blanket soft as cottonwood down,
settle into the sofa,
puzzle over the paper
like a Sphinx.

Sine Seeking

Like a longbow arrow,
I oscillate through space,
whip left and right
to correct my course.

Like a sustained note,
I quaver flat and sharp,
tremble my way to true pitch.

Like a timid poet,
I tiptoe at the edges of clarity—

but the musician knows better
how to stay in tune
riding vibrato waves

and the archer aims
to hit the mark,
understanding how the arrow
bends around the bow.

Saturday

Can't sleep.
Work on poem,
crossword puzzles,
solitaire in the dark.
Feed the dog.
Swallow pills
and buttered toast.
Dice peppers, onion;
fry sausage, beef.
Fill crockpot,
set on low.
Read:
      fiction,
      Facebook,
      news,
      rumors
Welcome sick child home from camp.
Send well child off to soccer.
Slice rolls.
Chill chicken salad.
Wash grapes.
Pick through lunch.
Work on poem.
Facebook again.
Nap.
Can't sleep.
New crossword hasn't loaded.
Pack food,
deliver to church.
Party:
      set up,
      chat,
      eat,
      laugh,
      games,
      clean up.

Home.
Pray.
Bed.
Can't sleep.
Return to impossible
poem.

Natural Born Poet

My heart beats out in iambs bold and strong.
My feet staccato trochees as I walk.
My thoughts compose like lyrics to a song
and words pour forth as free verse when I talk.

From abstract concepts weighing on my mind,
my eyes and ears make concrete metaphors.
I hear life's ancient timepiece slowly grind
and see my boat approach once distant shores.

Sometimes I halt through scansion set askew,
but though I seem enslaved, don't pity me.
The structure of a stanza keeps me true;
the rhyming of a couplet sets me free.

When youth bleeds dry and nothing else sustains,
pure poetry will still run through these veins.

On Turning 40

The clock hands used to stick,
poised in stasis on its face.
Students bent over desks
while seconds stretched so long
we thought they ticked
just once in five minutes.

The clockworks must have jammed:
springs gathered force
till something snapped,
spun me off through decades
of life at a leap.

I've skidded here to middle ground,
off-kilter and flailing.
My past folds in behind
like an accordion
of compressed memories
gathering momentum, threatening
to fling me forward again.

For a moment I stay,
survey the landscape,
plan my trajectory—
look for a way up
instead of over this hill.

Paper Boats

I make paper boats
to follow random currents,
slip silently down flooded gutters
into gaping storm drains,
whirl on backwater eddies.

I send them light and skipping—
ski boats ripping through dawn
across polished lakes.

I send them slow and still—
windless frigates foundering
on outcropped thoughts.

I send them budding and abundant—
flower flotillas spreading out
like green sea bloom.

I make paper boats
to ferry vital bits of me—
dark chocolate craving,
love of deep red,
eddying, centripetal faith—

because a hundred years downstream,
my grandchildren wait
for messages on the water.

Refraction

When every day
falls pale and faded,
meting light enough to see by
but no warmth

sometimes joy breaks—
a single beam sidelong
through water drop on window—
scattering bright ribbons
across my pillow

till earth shifts,
and each gleaming thread
gradually gathers,
reweaves into one.

As afternoon wears on
toward evening,
I'll pull out this small moment
to study and consider
how happiness stood still
and let me count its colors.

Nature

Anticipation

Spring simmers beneath the snow
like subterranean hot springs.
Earth shivers, shoots daffodil spikes
through late winter's crumbling crust.

New life is ready to blow,
shower the valley
with frothy white geysers
of apple blossoms.

For now,
spring simmers beneath the snow,
but in the bones of my feet
I feel the pressure
building.

Putting Up Peaches

Beside the garden wall where grapevines run,
a peach tree stands, diseased and bent with age.
Her blackened branches reach up to the sun
in daily supplication for her wage.

Each year, I think, must surely be her last,
but faithfulness is undeterred by whims.
So, not content to rest on harvests past,
she bears young fruit on geriatric limbs.

With every spring, new buds and blooms emerge
and swell with promise fed by summer rains.
Though twisted and decrepit, still the surge
of liquid light flows through her ancient veins.

When winter strips her bare, I'll be consoled
by pantry shelves stacked deep with jars of gold.

Human Nature

In the city,
glass-skinned buildings
like bitmapped mountains
pulse with interior stars.

Streets flow with headlights
like lambent corpuscles
navigating a maze
of webbed capillaries.

The neighborhood crawls
with progeny enough
to fascinate any ant-farm gazer.

Our house clings to earth
like mudded swallow's nest,
bright as bowerbird canopy
strewn with colored nothings.

My children, too,
push over the edge
like wild, young larks
falling into flight.

Easter Greetings

Sophisticated trees line State Street,
elegantly avoiding one another.
They pose
with thin, black limbs
silhouetted against the sky
and roots sunk deep
beneath concrete.

Up the canyon,
the rabble crowds in close.
Scrub oak brushes up to aspen groves,
listens for whispered rumors.
Expectation spreads with the wind,
rattles bone-weary stands,
stirs the lofty thoughts
of quorumed pines.
Sap rises, buds swell, branches reach
to embrace dawning spring.

Back in the city,
trees carefully dress for Easter,
nodding to the new sun
almost as an afterthought.

Come, Daddy Longlegs

Come, daddy longlegs, dance with me.
Whirl through the vines of the wild sweet pea.
Wearing our finest, we'll grandly pose
like ballerinas on tippy toes.

Come, lucky cricket, sing your song.
Kick out your feet as you skip along.
I'll start the round so you can reply,
echoing chirps through the cool night sky.

Come, silly pill bug, let's play ball.
Why do you creep up against the wall?
Tuck in your legs, take a running roll,
pass through the posts as I call out *Goal!*

Come, slinky snail, but take your time.
Paint me a picture in silver slime.
I'll work with mud while you supervise,
swaying the stalks of your knobby eyes.

Come, lacy mayfly, flit my way.
Let's make the most of your only day.
Time is the money I freely spend,
wishing and winging with you, my friend.

Serendipity

The sunset splashes honey colors wide
and floods the valley floor with golden light.
It laps the mountains on the other side
before it circles down the drain of night.

Upon the dark blue dusk, the moon floats high,
adrift within the last of twilight's glow.
Too early for the stars to fleck the sky,
the city lights take up the task below.

I'm one such light, now flowing through a stream
of weekday traffic like a shooting star.
By merest chance, I caught this evening's dream
because I had to navigate my car

from basketball to piano for my son.
Thank heaven for the errands I must run.

Earth Says

From foothills,
Earth spreads bare toes
into desert valley sand,
smooths red-gold skirt over mountain lap,
twists ribbons of morning mist and frost
across yellow field grass.
Come sit, Earth says.

So I stop:
Wood smoke on the wind threads
through damp, decaying garden.
Sluggish crickets creak a song
for brittle, brown zinnia bones'
rattle-crack dance.
Come sit, Earth says. *Rest*.

But I resist—to the north,
geese honk muted calls
to gather for lift off.
They rise in rolling v's
from pond to cloud-rippled blue.
Come fly, Sky says.
And I go.

To a Planet with Four Suns*

We are always searching:
hunter-gatherers of the heavens,
we scrape for crumbs
to fill our hunger.

We found you tucked
in God's back pocket,
jingling like a lost button
with four forgotten pennies.

Across five thousand light years
of dark, empty desert,
we thirst for your blazing oasis—
but you remain
distant.

So we search on:
upend the sky,
sift through spilled stars like sand,
look for other suns, worlds,
souls who yearn back.

* In 2012, astronomers discovered the first reported case of a planet
orbiting a pair of twin suns that in turn is orbited by a second distant
pair of stars.

Autumn Calls

Old autumn calls me like a long-lost friend,
inviting me to sit a spell at ease,
to rest my rusty bones at summer's end.

I take my leisure watching fall descend
and feel the earth relaxing by degrees.
Old autumn calls me like a long-lost friend,

and blows her leafy limbs as if to send
a kiss and bid me idle as I please,
Come rest your rusty bones at summer's end!

Though gold October brings a bitter trend
in weather, changing colors warm the breeze
as autumn calls me like a long-lost friend.

Tomorrow let the waning days portend
of dreariness and January freeze—
today I rest my bones at summer's end.

Then let me have an empty hour to spend
just stretching out beneath the yellow trees.
Old autumn calls me like a long-lost friend
to rest my rusty bones at summer's end.

Watching Basketball on a November Afternoon

As I bench-warm at playground's edge,
the woman next to me
drums delicate finger rhythms
on her newborn's back,
counterpoint to percussive thump
of ball on blacktop.

I rest my chin on fists,
consider colored chalk drawings
littering the ground like leaves
of leftover summer.

Warm sun persuades over my right shoulder;
chill shadow undercuts from the left.

Beyond the empty soccer field,
across fenced-out seas of gray-green weeds,
yellow poplars point emphatically up to blue,
unswayed by autumn wind's insufficient argument.

To the east,
rust-gold mountains recline,
wait for the inevitable.
Together we ponder the hustle and hurl
of rubber spheres across vacant sky.

Sunsets Missed

How many solemn sunsets did I miss
when I was two or three? It's only right
I can't recall the press of evening's kiss

from way back then. I felt no haunting loss,
for Mother rose my morning, set my night.
How many solemn sunsets did I miss

when I was just sixteen, so full of fuss
and intrigue, burning red at every slight?
I can't recall the press of evening's kiss,

but if *he* asked, I knew I'd answer, "Yes."
I even prayed to stars, "I wish he might."
How many solemn sunsets did I miss

when I was twenty-five? I would caress
instead my newborn's tiny fists balled tight.
I can't recall the press of evening's kiss

since, all my life, my orbit wrapped its pass
around some brighter sun, some whiter light.
How many solemn sunsets did I miss?
I can't recall the press of evening's kiss.

Tease

Black branches sag
beneath fresh snow as white
as blown cherry blossoms.

Sun-bright ice drips
from stiff tree limbs
like flowing sap.

Bluebottle sky strings out
cloud ribbons as clean
as line-dried sheets.

Brisk breezes scatter
powder like petals
over laughing children.

Winter mimics spring today.
Willingly,
I play along.

Introspection

After dark,
clouds wrap around the valley
like a white bowl turned over.
Veiled heaven reflects
city lights
inward.

I walk alone,
boots crunching
through snow.
Frozen breath hangs close—
tiny clouds caught
by my gravity.

I look up
searching for stars.
But tonight, heaven stays veiled
and every guiding light
reflects inward.

Family

Jacob brings me weeds—

flowers, he says—
sheltered in cupped hands
like snowflakes on death's edge:

white bindweed trumpets, bright
as thoughts popping,
winding vines that cling
like anxious fingers twisted
through mine—

yellow dandelion puffs, dusty
as mote-filled sunbeams,
heavy tops that bob
like drowsy heads dipped
nose-first into dreams—

purple henbit pixels, scattered
as random patches of forgotten fury,
scarlet buds that blush
like hot cheeks rashed
with frustration.

Too limp to prop in porcelain vase,
too small to float in crystal bowl,
I tuck these treasures into memory's tissue,
press them under leaves of leaden time
to fill empty space—

buffer
between now and when
he brings me other things
I don't know how to save.

Making Waves

I hurl my frantic days
like handfuls of gravel
on wind-driven waves.
Splashing and spitting,
they startle jittery, flint-scaled fish,
provoke muddy clouds,
sink to fitful sleep
beneath choppy water.

Just once,
I'd like to rise unrushed,
choose a smooth stone,
skip it with precision
across a patient lake.

I'd watch each distinct ring
ripple out, reverberate,
and return.

Sonnet for an Infant

It's long past midnight now—yet still I walk
the floor and sing these fruitless lullabies
to one small son who, heedless of the clock,
fills up the night with loud, persistent cries.

The tiny tyrant trumpets his desires
in oratories eloquent and deep.
It seems a hundred years before he tires
and lets me coax his weary soul to sleep.

What makes him so secure in his demands
that boldly he calls out into the night
for sustenance and reassuring hands,
well knowing I'll respond without a fight?

Perhaps he knows I'll do the things I do
because my love is blind at half-past two.

Adolescent

He's full of cornered shelves,
crammed cubbies,
drawers ajar and spilling over—
not quite fitting or filling
his space.
I want to shake him out—
wipe away the dust,
puzzle together a complete picture,
display all his shining moments,
matted and framed.

He deposits life
in sedimentary layers—
slick seashells and broken stones,
pencil stubs and smudged drawings,
whorled marbles and worn coins.
I itch to sort through the pieces,
polish and set a jeweled mosaic,
excavate the unrefined ore
biding its precious time
just beneath his surface.

I gather myself to enter
his edifice under construction,
tour the premises,
admire the vaulted ceilings,
nudge a beam square here and there—
but I hover, undecided,
an ignorant visitor stuttering
and stumbling outside his door,
not grasping how to unlatch
the unknown.

Stillborn

You were wanted,
not an accident.

Your first fluttering cells
set plans pulsing—
names, knitting, nursery colors,
universities.

Though two others came before,
I saved a part for you.

Sometimes a heart stops beating
and dreams bleed free
in a slow, red river
of barren pain.

No healing prayers,
no reasons sought,
none given.
Just one of those things.

But it wasn't an accident.
You were wanted
elsewhere.

Mother

You haven't left yet,
but when you do
I'll remind the children how you
made sandwiches on warm wheat bread,
stocked popsicles in your outdoor freezer,
filled closets with homemade quilts.

I'll tell them old stories
of you pacing restless nights away,
waiting for flown teenagers.
Mothers never sleep well, you'd say.

I'll show them how to make
hand-pulled honey candy
from notes I scratched out
that day I called you, craving.

I'll teach them how to scrape
buttery flesh from artichoke leaves,
lift pastry sheets untorn into bed,
fill strawberry pots with petunias, phlox, asters—
anything but strawberries.

I'll sing them up mornings,
kneel them down evenings,
fast them full, pray them safe
each breathing moment.

But even if I squeeze out
every drop you poured into me,
those bitter-sweet juices
can only flow so long.

So when you go,
leave the door ajar.
Peek in while we sleep,

whisper reminders
of how to measure hems straight
and the best way to comfort
newborn puppies.

Moment

My little one crouches—
blue eyes fixed on a honey bee
busily picking clean a purple crocus bowl—
glances back to make sure I'm watching.

Our eyes meet and we smile,
happy to be busy at nothing.

Sister

You swallow sorrow
like knives slicing
down to your heart.

I want to gather you,
press the pieces together,
stanch the bleeding—

but I fear you like
a wounded animal.
Will you whimper or snarl,
snap or cower,
cringe at my touch?

I circle,
reach out,
offer my crumbs,

try to slip in
and shift the burden
sideways.

In Training

He digs,
scoops moist, sandy holes to hold the sea,
tunnels through snow mounds hollowed
into eggshell caverns.

He molds,
rolls clay solar systems in his hands,
shapes mud-colored bars
into sinuous snakes.

He builds,
stacks precarious towers of wooden blocks,
snaps slick plastic bricks
into stepped pyramids and treacherous spans.

He surveys,
stands over still life laid out in pithy detail,
views chaos harnessed and trained
into organized disorder.

He smiles,
turns quick eyes up to mine,
Is it good? he asks.
Very good, I say.

He nods,
bears kisses with dignity,
gathers himself for prayers, tucked covers,
and dreams of another day.

Ghost

On black nights fat with dreams,
I wake in lucid spaces,
listen to the house crack and settle
while midnight traffic moans outside
like vagrant wraiths rushing
from past to future.

I used to walk with you
wrapped in my arms,
wailing bundle of promises.
Now I creak past your door
as you sleep wrapped
in solitary visions.

I was your sun,
now a distant star
washed faint by city lights.
I was rumbling thunder,
now a murmur
drowned by clamorous crowds.

When sky grays toward morning,
you will resurrect, arise.
I will fade into the photographs,
insubstantial as an afterthought.

But in quiet interludes,
let me haunt the corners of your mind,
linger behind consciousness
like the perfect words
hanging just beyond
the tip of your tongue.

Sunset

Stretching out my legs,
I lean against the porch steps,
content to watch my four sons
wrestle in the long grass.
They tangle and laugh,
sprawling with limbs flung
across the lawn.

On the horizon,
the sun leans against the sandstone sky
and slips her rays into the lake.
She glows across the valley,
gilding rooftops red-gold
and stretching long shadows
through darkened backyards.
A breeze tousles the lawn,
ruffling leggy, half-blown dandelions.

My boys' faces shine
as soft and fair as early morning.
Like wild yellow flowers,
they race to the light
with no fear of harvest.

I shiver—
the warm wind has stilled.
Soon the setting sun
will draw the shade of night
down behind her,
chasing us all indoors
to warm beds, prayers,
and hope of dawn.

Like love,

you can only write so many poems
about the sky—

whether saturated with slate-blue clouds,
heavy as huddled bison herds
in leisurely migration
over valley grazing grounds,

or dry and flat
as bone china crisply glazed,
as lead crystal glinting
so it seems to ping
when first light hits—

but every time I look up,
heaven grabs hold and lifts,
pumps my heart as full
as a helium balloon, and I think:
This should be a poem.

Just like when you walk by
raining unexpected kisses
across my upturned face.

Notes

Some of the poems in this book were inspired by or allude to scriptures found in the four standard works of The Church of Jesus Christ of Latter-day Saints: The Holy Bible, The Book of Mormon, The Doctrine and Covenants, and The Pearl of Great Price. These poems are listed below in alphabetical order, along with their page numbers in this book and scripture references.

For your convenience, you can access digital copies of the standard works online at www.lds.org/scriptures.

* These poems have been set to music by Jennette Jay Booth. To find copies of the music online, visit www.soundboothstudios.com.

About the Author

Merrijane Rice grew up in Bountiful, Utah. She received a B.A. in English from Brigham Young University and later served a mission for The Church of Jesus Christ of Latter-day Saints in Washington, D.C. She currently works as a technical writer and editor for DMBA. She and her husband Jason are raising four sons in Kaysville, Utah.

For inquiries about this publication, email Merrijane at merrijane.rice@gmail.com.